THE
Student Bible Guide to Jerusalem

By Robert Backhouse

Jerusalem by night, from the Mount of Olives.

CANDLE BOOKS

The Old City, Jerusalem

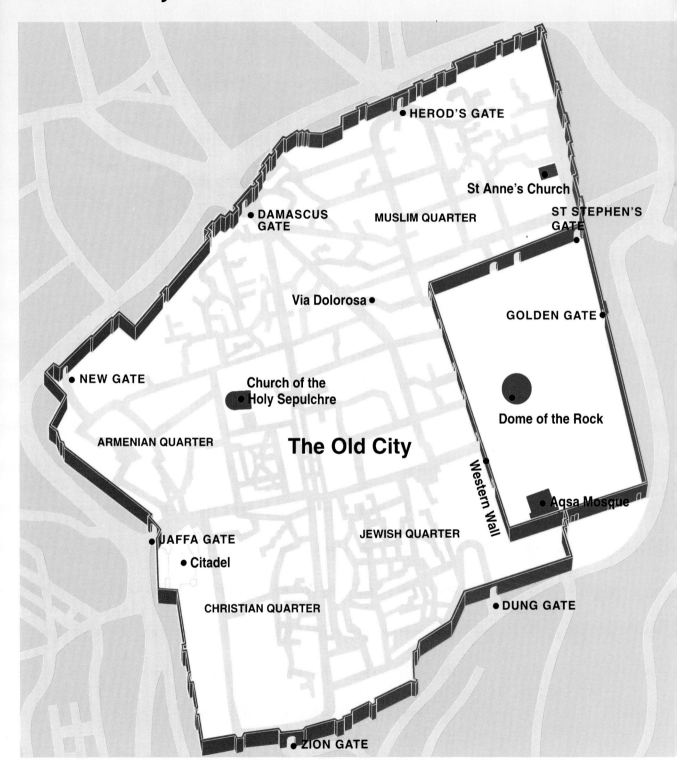

HEROD'S GATE

St Anne's Church

MUSLIM QUARTER

ST STEPHEN'S GATE

DAMASCUS GATE

Via Dolorosa

GOLDEN GATE

NEW GATE

Church of the Holy Sepulchre

Dome of the Rock

ARMENIAN QUARTER

The Old City

Western Wall

JAFFA GATE

Citadel

JEWISH QUARTER

Aqsa Mosque

CHRISTIAN QUARTER

DUNG GATE

ZION GATE

Scale

0 metres   300

Contents

A mosaic showing Jerusalem in the Byzantine period.

King David's City

Palestine

JERUSALEM

Jerusalem – the city of David, Solomon's showcase, the scene of Jesus' last week on earth – is also a holy place of Islam, and the goal of both medieval Crusaders and modern pilgrims.

The first time Jerusalem is named in the Bible is when Abraham met Melchizedek, a mysterious king from Salem (Jerusalem), who blessed the patriarch (Genesis 14:18-20). Egyptian records – the 'Execration Texts', from as far back as the 19th century BC – probably refer to Jerusalem, as do 14th century BC clay tablets found in Tell el-Amarna, central Egypt, known as the Amarna Letters.

When the Israelites entered the Promised Land, they failed to drive the Jebusites from their fortified town of Jebus (Jerusalem). After David became ruler of the united kingdom of Judah and Israel, he needed a new capital city. Jerusalem was ideally positioned, belonging to neither of the two jealous kingdoms. David's commander, Joab, led a successful assault on Jerusalem, which now became known as 'the City of David' (2 Samuel 5:6-10).

An artist's impression of Jerusalem in the time of King David.

Tunnelling into Jerusalem

The Jebusites boasted that Jerusalem – perched on the top of a hill with three steep sides – could never be captured. They taunted David, 'You will not get in here; even the blind and the lame can ward you off' (2 Samuel 5:6). But David took Jerusalem by surprise when his men climbed a water-shaft which tunnelled beneath the city walls.

King David strengthened Jerusalem's fortifications, and brought the Ark of the Covenant to the city, making it the political and religious centre for God's people. David bought a threshing floor from the Jebusite Araunah and on its site built an altar of sacrifice (2 Samuel 24:13-25). By tradition this is also Mount Moriah, where Abraham so nearly sacrificed his son Isaac (Genesis 22:2). Jerusalem's most important building, the Temple, was to be built on exactly the same site (2 Chronicles 3:1-2).

Solomon Builds the Temple

King Solomon, David's son, greatly famed for his wisdom, strengthened Jerusalem. He extended the city northwards, employed a permanent army to protect his land and capital city, made shrewd peace treaties with neighbouring countries and became fabulously wealthy, by controlling lucrative trade routes (2 Chronicles 9:13). Solomon truly put Jerusalem on the map.

Solomon's crowning achievement was not his sumptuous palace but the Temple, which took seven years to build. Solomon made full use of the site, plans and preparations which David had made for this place of worship and sacrifice.

The interior of the Temple was based on the two-room design of the movable Tabernacle (Tent of Meeting) which it replaced. Dwarfed by the two pillars standing at the Temple entrance, Jachin ('he will establish') on the right, and Boaz ('in strength') on the left, the priest entered into the first room, the Holy Place,

Solomon's Temple was built of pure white limestone, the interior wall panelled in choice cedar from the Lebanon's mountain forests.

1. Holiest Place
2. Holy Place
3. Jachin
4. Boaz
5. Ark of the Covenant

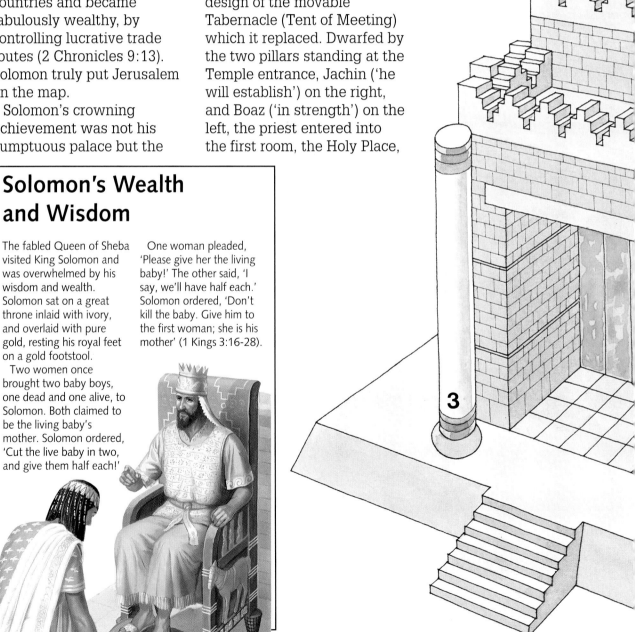

Solomon's Wealth and Wisdom

The fabled Queen of Sheba visited King Solomon and was overwhelmed by his wisdom and wealth. Solomon sat on a great throne inlaid with ivory, and overlaid with pure gold, resting his royal feet on a gold footstool.

Two women once brought two baby boys, one dead and one alive, to Solomon. Both claimed to be the living baby's mother. Solomon ordered, 'Cut the live baby in two, and give them half each!'

One woman pleaded, 'Please give her the living baby!' The other said, 'I say, we'll have half each.' Solomon ordered, 'Don't kill the baby. Give him to the first woman; she is his mother' (1 Kings 3:16-28).

through a massive set of folding olive-wood doors, to discover ten golden lampstands, the tables of showbread and an altar of incense.

The second room, the Holiest Place (Holy of Holies), was a perfect cube, measuring 20 x 20 x 20 cubits. Gold was everywhere. Solomon overlaid the inside with 20 tons of fine gold. Each gold nail weighed 0.6 kg – 11/4lb (see 2 Chronicles 3:1-17).

The temple courtyard was no less spectacular, with its ten washing basins mounted on wheels, and the massive bronze tank, or laver, supported on twelve huge bronze oxen. This tank was two metres (seven feet) deep, four and a half metres (15 feet) in diameter and 13 metres (40 feet) in circumference. Once the animals had been cleansed here, they were sacrificed on the nine-metre (30-foot) square bronze altar.

An artist's impression of the Ark of the Covenant.

Did You Know?

Solomon used forced labour to build the Temple, including:

- 80,000 stonecutters
- 70,000 porters to transport the dressed stone
- 30,000 men to transport cedar wood from Lebanon
- 3,000 foremen to supervise the work

Besieged, Destroyed, Rebuilt

Jerusalem reached its greatest glory under Solomon. There followed a pattern of decline, siege, surrender, deportation, repatriation and rebuilding.

In 917 BC King Shishak of Egypt came to Jerusalem, plundering 'everything' from the treasures of the Temple (2 Chronicles 12:9). Later, Jerusalem suffered famine when the Assyrian King Sennacherib laid siege to Jerusalem and shut up King Hezekiah 'like a bird in a cage'. The Bible records an amazing escape: 'That night an angel of the LORD went to the Assyrian camp and killed 185,000 soldiers. At dawn the next day, there they lay, all dead! Then the Assyrian emperor Sennacherib withdrew and returned to Nineveh' (2 Kings 19:20-37).

Between the reign of Solomon and Jerusalem's destruction by King Nebuchadnezzar in 587 BC Jerusalem was plundered eight times. The last king of Judah in Jerusalem, Zedekiah, was placed in chains and taken to Babylon (2 Kings 25:1-21), along with the Temple treasures.

Exile and return

For seventy years the Israelites languished in Babylon, with their own beloved city and Temple in ruins. Then King Cyrus of Persia issued an edict allowing the Temple to be rebuilt. Gradually, Jerusalem was repopulated. Sheshbazzar was made Governor of Judah in 537 BC; then Zerubbabel and Joshua led more exiles back to Jerusalem in 525 BC; as did Nehemiah, and Ezra in 428 BC. Nehemiah inspected the broken-down walls of Jerusalem and rebuilt them. 'After fifty-two days of work the entire wall was finished' (Nehemiah 2:1-20; 6:15).

Exile

Return

King Jehoiachin and the leading citizens of Jerusalem were exiled by Nebuchadnezzar in 597 BC, followed by the rest of the able-bodied people, with King Zedekiah, in 586 BC. The exiles returned to Jerusalem in waves, under Sheshbazzar, Zerubbabel, Joshua, Nehemiah and Ezra, from 537 BC to 428 BC.

Jerusalem

Babylon

Nehemiah supervises the rebuilding of the walls of Jerusalem *c.* 427 BC.

Herod the Great

Herod the Great, renowned for his cruelty and ambition

The fortress of Herodium, built by Herod the Great near Bethlehem.

Herod the Great was infamous for his cruel-heartedness. He murdered his son and expected heir, Antipater, five days before he died himself. History also remembers him for his lavish building programmes.

Herod rebuilt the temple at Samaria, 'out of a desire to make the city more eminent than it had been before, but principally because he contrived that it might at once be for his own security and a monument of his magnificence' (Josephus). He renamed Samaria Sebaste (meaning Augustus), and built a theatre and forum as well as a temple dedicated to Augustus.

Herod made Caesarea his capital, and built impressive breakwaters and a vast artificial harbour measuring 500 metres (550 yards) by 270 metres (300 yards), making it into an impressive new port.

Impregnable

King Herod also built an impregnable fortress and summer retreat at Masada, which included two lavish palaces, and his own private bath – with its changing room, cold plunge bath, warm room and hot room – as well as a public bathhouse. At Herodium, near Bethlehem, he built a walled fortress on a hill-top, with four towers to protect it, from which heavy catapults could fire on any besieging force.

But Herod carried out his most ambitious building programme in Jerusalem. He

Cleansing the Temple

A great struggle arose during the reign of Antiochus IV Epiphanes (175-163 BC), the Seleucid ruler of the Jews. His Jewish subjects were determined to retain their distinctive life and religion; the Seleucid king was equally determined to make Jerusalem a city in the Greek style. The Jews resisted fanatically when pigs (unclean animals for Jews) were offered in sacrifice on Jerusalem's new Greek altars, and the Temple rededicated to the Greek god Zeus. Judas, nicknamed 'the Hammer', led a Jewish guerrilla war, known as the Maccabean Revolt, from the hills surrounding Jerusalem.

Surprisingly, the Seleucids were eventually forced to accept the terms demanded by the Jews. The Temple was reinstated as the focus of Jewish worship and on 14 December 164 BC, after ritual cleansing, it was rededicated (1 Maccabees 4:36-59). This is celebrated annually by the Jews at the festival of *Chanukah*.

Judas' successors now ruled as the Hasmoneans, and successfully governed Jerusalem until the Romans, under Pompey, captured the city in 63 BC. King Herod the Great was a Hasmonean, but was primarily interested in retaining his throne, as he showed when he ordered the slaughter of all the boy children in Bethlehem.

A special *Chanukah* candlestick.

The Tomb of the Herod family.

Above: Robinson's arch, part of the structure remaining from Herod's Temple.
Below: A model of Herodian Jerusalem, showing the hippodrome.

remodelled the *Baris* (fortress) north of the Temple, renaming it the 'Antonia Fortress' in honour of Mark Antony. He built a second fortress, with three massive towers, on the western side of Jerusalem, his Upper Palace linking the two fortresses with a great wall. Herod also built himself a more modest Lower Palace in the centre of Jerusalem.

Far-reaching

Herod also constructed in Jerusalem baths, a theatre, and a hippodrome, or stadium, where he promoted both Greek and Roman games. Two existing pools, just beyond the north-east corner of the Temple area, Herod replaced with the larger Pool of Israel.

Herod's far-reaching building programme for Jerusalem meant that the street plan for the city had to be changed. Jerusalem changed little after his death in 4 BC, before it was levelled by the Romans in AD 70.

Herod's Temple

Herod crowned his extensive building programme in Jerusalem with the magnificent Temple, built of cream-coloured stone and decorated with gold. He hoped to gain the favour of his Jewish subjects by reconstructing the Temple and making it one of the Wonders of the World. He began rebuilding the Temple in Jerusalem in 20 BC, and although he finished the main building by AD 9, the outer courts were not completed until AD 64.

Herod first made a massive 35-acre platform for the Temple and its surrounding courts. The Temple court was surrounded by a portico, or covered porch. The central Temple buildings were approached by impressive steps, giving access to the Court of the Women, beyond which women were prohibited.

An artist's impression of Herod's Temple.

1. **Altar of Sacrifice**
2. **Laver**
3. **Court of Priests**
4. **Nicanor Gate**
5. **Court of Women**
6. **The Beautiful Gate**

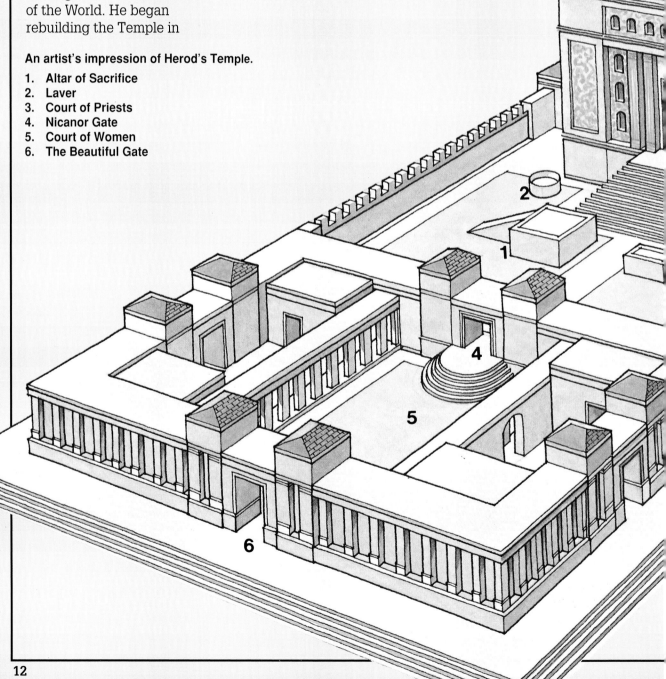

In the Court of the Priests stood the laver, a massive bowl provided for washing the animals, and the raised altar where they were sacrificed. John the Baptist's first recorded words about Jesus in John's Gospel were, 'Look, the Lamb of God, who takes away the sin of the world!' (John 1:29). The Temple and the sacrificial system was completely fulfilled in Jesus, 'the lamb of God'.

Inside the first room of the Temple, the Holy Place, the priests burned incense. The Holiest Place (the Holy of Holies, the sacred inner room), was empty, since the Ark of the Covenant had disappeared when Solomon's Temple was ransacked centuries earlier. The building was the equivalent of fifteen stories high, and the floor dimensions of the two rooms were similar to those of Solomon's Temple.

Model of Herod's Temple.

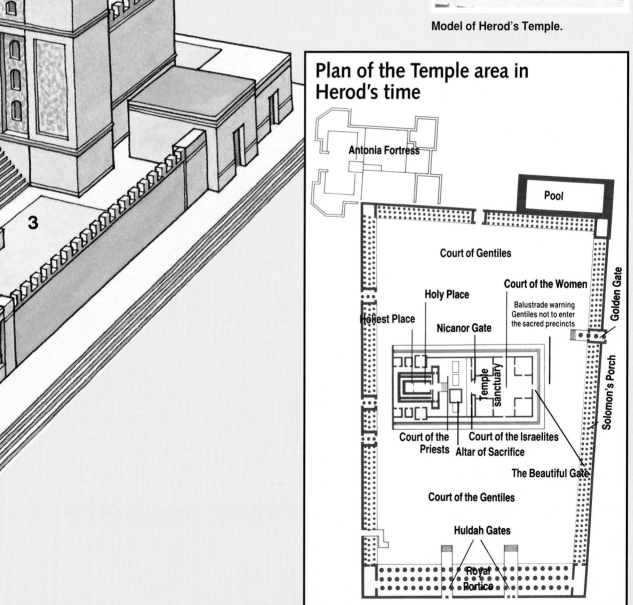

Plan of the Temple area in Herod's time

Antonia Fortress

Pool

Court of Gentiles

Holy Place

Court of the Women

Holiest Place

Nicanor Gate

Balustrade warning Gentiles not to enter the sacred precincts

Golden Gate

Temple sanctuary

Solomon's Porch

Court of the Priests

Court of the Israelites

Altar of Sacrifice

The Beautiful Gate

Court of the Gentiles

Huldah Gates

Royal Portico

3

Jesus' Love for Jerusalem

Jesus knew that Jerusalem was a special city, with God's Temple at its heart. He loved Jerusalem, its people and all it stood for. As he came near to Jerusalem, Jesus 'wept over it' (Luke 19:41). He said, 'Jerusalem! . . . How many times have I wanted to put my arms round all your people, just as a hen gathers her chicks under her wings' (Luke 13:34).

The twelve-year-old Jesus

All Jewish men were expected to visit the Temple in Jerusalem for the three major Jewish festivals: the Feast of Passover, the Feast of Weeks and the Feast of Tabernacles. At the age of twelve, Jesus came from Nazareth to Jerusalem with Mary and Joseph to celebrate Passover. Jerusalem was

The Old City of Jerusalem viewed from the Mount of Olives. The Golden Gate may be seen in front of the Dome of the Rock.

Muslims outside the Dome of the Rock.

An Orthodox Jew at the Western Wall.

Jews at prayer at the Western Wall.

crowded with pilgrims from throughout the Roman Empire.

Mary and Joseph lost Jesus for three days, but eventually found him in the Temple courts. He was sitting with the learned teachers of the Jewish faith, listening to them and asking them questions. 'All who heard Jesus were amazed at his intelligent answers' (see Luke 2:41-52).

Jesus clears the Temple

As a grown man, Jesus visited Jerusalem just before the Passover. In the Temple courts he found men selling cattle, sheep and doves. He saw others sitting at tables acting as currency exchangers, changing ordinary coins for the special silver coins needed by pilgrims as Temple tax.

Jesus was very angry. He made a whip out of cords, and used it to drive them from the Temple. He overturned the traders' tables, saying 'How dare you make my Father's house into a market' (John 2:13-17).

Outside the Church of the Holy Sepulchre.

Jesus' Last Week in Jerusalem

Many times Jesus foretold his death in Jerusalem. 'I must go to Jerusalem and suffer much from the elders, the chief priests, and the teachers of the Law. I will be put to death, but three days later I will be raised to life' (Matthew 16:21, GNB).

The last week of Jesus' life was spent in and around Jerusalem. It started triumphantly. As Jesus entered Jerusalem, humbly riding a colt, a crowd of disciples spread their coats on the ground, while others cut branches from trees and spread them on the ground. They shouted out in welcome, 'Hosanna to the Son of David! Blessed is the king who comes in the name of the Lord!' (see Matthew 21:1-11).

The chief priests, elders and high priest, Caiaphas – Jerusalem's religious leaders – plotted to 'arrest Jesus in some sly way and kill him', but they were afraid of causing a riot, as Jesus was so popular (see Matthew 26:1-5).

The Garden Tomb, a tranquil haven.

Last Supper

Jesus celebrated the Jewish Passover meal with his disciples in secret in the first-floor room of a Jerusalem house. He broke bread, saying: 'This is my body.' He then passed round a cup of wine, saying, 'This is my blood' (Matthew 26:17-30).

The Mount of Olives from Jerusalem. *Left to right*: The Church of All Nations, the Russian Church of St Mary Magdalene and the Chapel of Dominus Flevit.

The Golden Gate viewed from the garden of Gethsemane.

Via Dolorosa

Via Dolorosa
In modern Jerusalem the *Via Dolorosa* (Latin for 'the way of suffering') marks the possible route of Jesus' journey from the place where the Roman governor, Pilate, condemned him to death, to the place of his crucifixion and burial. At each of the 14 'stations' (the Gospels mention eight) there is a church or inscription reminding us of some aspect of Christ's Passion.

The garden of Gethsemane

After supper Jesus and eleven disciples (Judas, the betrayer, had left to arrange Jesus' arrest) went out to the east side of Jerusalem to the Mount of Olives. On the west slope lay the garden of Gethsemane, where Jesus loved to pray in a peaceful olive grove.

Jerusalem Annihilated

The First Jewish War

Tensions between the Roman administration in Jerusalem and the Jews led to a Jewish revolt in AD 66-70. Historians record how the Jews courageously tried to oppose the Roman army as it besieged Jerusalem. But the city and its Temple were reduced to rubble when the Jews continued to resist stubbornly.

The Second Jewish War

To try to prevent the Emperor Hadrian rebuilding Jerusalem as a Roman colony, Simon Bar-Kokhba led the Jews into the disastrous Second Jewish War, AD 132. Over 750,000 people were said to have been killed, and those Jews who were not killed were enslaved.

Jewish coin of the Second Jewish War, showing the facade of Herod's Temple.

Prophecy Fulfilled

One day, when Jesus and his disciples were in the Temple courts in Jerusalem, Jesus made two staggering prophecies about Jerusalem. Referring to his death and resurrection, he said, 'tear down this Temple, and in three days I will build it again' (John 2:18-22, GNB).

'Some of the disciples were talking about the Temple, how beautiful it looked with its fine stones . . . Jesus said, "All this you see – the time will come when not a single stone here will be left in its place; every one will be thrown down"' (Luke 21:5-6, GNB).

The destruction of Jerusalem and the Temple by the Roman commander Titus, with 70,000 soldiers from the Fifth, Tenth and Fifteenth Legions, in AD 70, happened in fulfilment of Jesus' prophecy.

An artist's impression of the Roman assault on the Antonia Fortress and the Temple Mount area.

Facts to Remember

THE JEWS AND JERUSALEM
● After the Second Jewish War no Jew was allowed into Jerusalem.
● The Romans changed Jerusalem's name to Aelia Capitolina.

The Pilgrims

Throughout the Christian era pilgrims have visited the Holy Land to view the Sea of Galilee, to visualise Jesus speaking to the crowds on the hillside, and to visit such places as Nazareth, Bethlehem and above all Jerusalem, so closely linked with Jesus' life. Such journeys have been made by every generation since Alexander, a friend of the Christian writer Origen, first set out in AD 212 'on a search after the footsteps of Jesus, the disciples and the prophets'.

The Empress Helena, Constantine the Great's mother, went on a pilgrimage to Jerusalem in AD 326 and in a quarry found wood which was reputed to be from the 'True Cross'. She built a number of churches in Jerusalem, one being the Church of the Holy Sepulchre, on the spot where she found the wood supposedly from Jesus' cross. Helena's pilgrimage to Jerusalem helped to make Jerusalem a Christian holy city.

Pilgrims still come to Jerusalem from all over the world, especially at Easter.

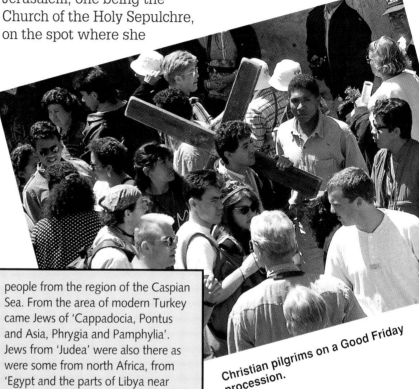

Christian pilgrims on a Good Friday procession.

The Chapel of the Ascension.

Jewish pilgrims

At Pentecost, the birthday of the Christian Church, Jerusalem was crowded with pilgrims: 'Now there were staying in Jerusalem God-fearing Jews from every nation under heaven.'

Luke emphasises the international nature of these pilgrims. There were 'Parthians, Medes and Elamites; residents of Mesopotamia' – that is people from the region of the Caspian Sea. From the area of modern Turkey came Jews of 'Cappadocia, Pontus and Asia, Phrygia and Pamphylia'. Jews from 'Judea' were also there as were some from north Africa, from 'Egypt and the parts of Libya near Cyrene'. Then there were visitors from Rome and lastly 'Cretans and Arabs' (Acts 2:5-9). 3,000 of these Jews became Christian converts on the Day of Pentecost (Acts 2:41).

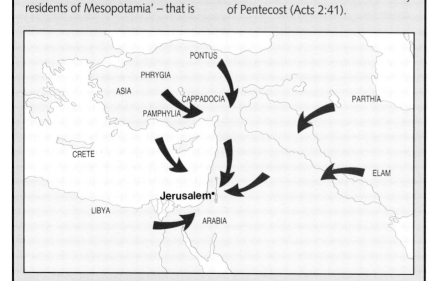

Jesus' last journey

Many want to follow in the steps of the last journey Jesus made along the *Via Dolorosa*.

At 3.00 on Good Friday pilgrims gather at **Station 1**, where Pontius Pilate condemned Jesus to death (Matthew 27:22-26). **Station 2** is where Jesus took up his cross (John 19:16-17); **Stations 3, 7** and **9** are places where Jesus collapsed under the weight of the cross, **Station 4** where Jesus met his mother, Mary, and **Station 5** where Simon of Cyrene took up Jesus' cross (Matthew 27:32).

Station 6, not mentioned in the Bible, is the traditional place when Veronica held her *sudarium* (Latin for handkerchief) to wipe Jesus' perspiring face.

Station 8 is where Jesus comforted the women of Jerusalem who were weeping for him, **Station 10** where Jesus was stripped of his clothes (Matthew 27:35), and **Station 11** where he was nailed to the cross (John 19:18).

The last three stations are in the Church of the Holy Sepulchre: **Station 12** where Jesus died on the cross (John 19:30), **Station 13** where he was taken down from the cross, and **Station 14** where his body was buried in the unused tomb (Matthew 27:60).

Above: At Easter many pilgrims come to the Church of the Holy Sepulchre to remember Christ's death and resurrection.

Below: Pilgrims travel to Jerusalem from all over the world for the Easter festivals.

The Crusaders

After the Roman Empire was divided up in AD 395, Jerusalem came under Byzantine rule. In 638 the Muslim Caliph Omar I captured Jerusalem and declared the Temple Mount a sacred place of Islam. Jerusalem now became an Islamic holy city.

In 1099 Pope Urban II launched the First Crusade to attempt to wrest control of the holy places from the Muslims. Some of the knights who went on these Crusades (there were eight in all) were like monks in armour, one moment showing Christian compassion for the poor – the next slaughtering their enemies in the most bloodthirsty way.

Holy War

The campaign for the capture of Jerusalem became a holy war. Godfrey of Bouillon led the First Crusade and captured Jerusalem, butchering more than 70,000 Jews and Muslims, and naming himself 'Defender of the Holy Sepulchre'. In 1100 he was succeeded by his brother, Baldwin I, crowned king of Jerusalem. Jerusalem was declared a 'Christian' city.

Once in control of Jerusalem, the Crusaders attempted to Christianise the city by erecting new buildings in honour of Christ. The Church of the Holy Sepulchre was restored, and the Crusaders converted the Dome of the Rock into a church which they named '*Templum Domini*' ('Temple of the Lord').

St Anne's Church, built by the Crusaders after taking Jerusalem.

Saladin

The Muslim leader Saladin, the founder of the Ayyub dynasty and Sultan of Egypt and Syria, became the famed adversary of the Christian Crusaders. He eventually succeeded in recapturing Jerusalem.

The German king and Holy Roman Emperor, Frederick II mounted a further Crusade in 1228, taking advantage of divisions among the Muslims. He managed to 'liberate' Jerusalem and Bethlehem. Nevertheless, the Muslims retained control of the Temple Mount.

In 1244 the Christians were finally driven out of Jerusalem, and in 1260 the Muslim Mamelukes took control of the city.

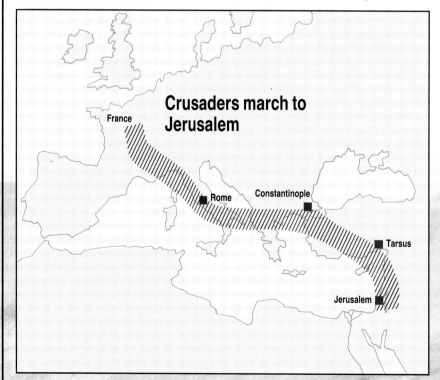

Crusaders march to Jerusalem

France

Rome

Constantinople

Tarsus

Jerusalem

Facts to remember

● The Crusaders formed a 'Kingdom of Jerusalem' lasting from 1099 to 1187, from Turkey to the Red Sea.
● They barred Muslims and Jews from Jerusalem.
● The Church of the Holy Sepulchre as we know it was dedicated in 1149.

An artist's impression of the assault on a gate of Jerusalem by the army of the Crusaders.

Islam's Holy City

After Mecca and Medina, Jerusalem's Dome of the Rock is the third holiest Islamic site. Islamic tradition says that the rock inside the Dome of the Rock is the point from which the prophet Mohammed started his journey to heaven on his miraculous horse *el-Buraq*.

The Dome of the Rock

The Dome of the Rock (*Qubbet es-Sakhra*) symbolises Islam's presence in Jerusalem. Its golden dome, crowning an

The Dome of the Rock.

The Dome of the Rock and Old City from the Mount of Olives.

24

octagonal base, is today Jerusalem's most famous landmark. Inside the dome is a rock outcrop traced back to Mount Moriah, where Abraham so nearly sacrificed his son Isaac. There are also tile and mosaic masterpieces of Islamic art from the time of Suleiman the Magnificent.

The dome itself is 23 metres (78 feet) in diameter and 53 metres (177 feet) high, topped with a 3.5 metre (12 foot) crescent.

Damascus Gate

The 15 metre (45 foot) high Damascus Gate is the largest and most impressive gate into the Old City of Jerusalem. It is also the most beautiful, with its decorations, battlements and turrets. It leads out of the Old City into Arab East Jerusalem. The Turkish ruler Suleiman the Magnificent left an indelible mark on Jerusalem with the impressive walls and gates he built around the Old City, c. AD 1517.

The Return of the Jews

Opposite: Jewish men pray at the Western Wall. The Torah scrolls are in the decorated case.

The Jews have always thought of Jerusalem as their holy city. They called it 'the city of David' after their most illustrious ancestor, who captured Jerusalem and made it the centre of worship by bringing in the Ark of the Covenant.

Every faithful Jew, echoing the words of the Psalmist, would 'pray for the peace of Jerusalem' (Psalm 122:6). Sadly, for many centuries Jews were prevented, first by the Romans, then by the Muslims, from setting foot inside Jerusalem, although they never stopped believing that God would save Zion (Psalm 69:35).

Birthright

The Jews never lost sight of the fact that the Holy Land was their birthright, and Jerusalem, God's city, belonged to them by right. During the 300 years following the Ottoman Sultan Suleiman the Magnificent's capture of Jerusalem in 1517, the Turks kept Jews out of the city.

Jerusalem opened again to the Jews in 1831, when Ibrahim Pasha of Egypt took the city and introduced liberalising reforms. Jews from all over the world, especially from Eastern Europe, trickled back to Jerusalem. The return of the Jews to the Old City changed its character.

In 1917 Sir Edmund Allenby led British troops into Jerusalem, after capturing it from the Turks. Jerusalem was now ruled by a high commissioner, under the British Mandate of Palestine. By 1946 Jews made up over 50 per cent of the population, with Muslims and Christians making up most of the rest of the population.

Facts to Remember

● God promised that Jerusalem would always be ruled by Jews (2 Samuel 7:16).
● Jews saw Jerusalem as 'the city of our God' which God had established for ever (Psalm 48:8).
● Jews knew that God loved his city (Psalm 87:2) and their greatest delight was to attend the temple in Jerusalem (Psalm 122:1).

The Western Wall

The Western Wall (*Kotel haMa'aravi*), also known as the Wailing Wall, is the only major part of the Jerusalem Temple to survive the devastation of the Romans in AD 70. It stands roughly 20 metres (65 feet) above the ground and has 19 layers of stonework below ground. At the bottom are beautifully cut stones which have survived from Herod's Temple enclosure.

The Western Wall is the most sacred Jewish site in the world. It formed part of the wall surrounding Herod's Temple.

Today Jewish families come to the Wester Wall to hold *Bar Mitzvahs* (literally meaning 'son of the commandment') for their young sons. Before dawn and throughout the day, Jews in traditional dress pray at the Western Wall. Jewish brides and grooms also come here to pray after they are married, still dressed in their wedding clothes.

An elderly Jew at the Western Wall.

Jerusalem Reborn

Sixty years ago even the most devout and optimistic Jew could hardly have believed that his people would regain their homeland, from which they had been exiled for so many centuries, and that Jerusalem would once again became the capital of Israel. Prior to 1947, the Jews were scattered over the face of the earth, but had no country which belonged to them and which they could call their own.

This all changed in 1948. The State of Israel came into existence, the British left Jerusalem, Jordan captured the Old City and the rest of Jerusalem was divided between Jordan and the Israelis.

During the remarkable Six Day War in June of 1967, the Israelis stormed the Old City (East Jerusalem, which belonged to Jordan) and claimed that Jerusalem was once again united. Even though the United Nations passed a resolution disapproving of this action, the whole of Jerusalem continued to be run by the Israelis as a united city.

In 1980 the *Knesset*, the Israeli parliament, made Jerusalem the official capital of Israel, much to the annoyance of the Arab countries surrounding Israel.

The *Mea Shearim* quarter of Jerusalem is home for many Orthodox Jews. Here the Ten Commandments are kept to the letter, and any car travelling through on the Sabbath is liable to be stoned.

Many of the landmarks of modern Jerusalem evoke the Jews' history of struggle against the odds, and of God's protecting hand on them. The Shrine of the Book, with its distinctive roof in the shape of the top of a clay pot, symbolising the pots containing the leather and papyrus scrolls found at

A modern suburb of Jerusalem, viewed from Yad Vashem, the Holocaust memo

The *Knesset*, the Israeli Parliament.

The Shrine of the Book, specially built to house some of the Dead Sea Scrolls.

Qumran, houses some of the Dead Sea Scrolls, which include early copies of the Old Testament scriptures.

The stark Holocaust Memorial *Yad Vashem* pays sombre homage to the six million Jews exterminated by the Nazis during the Second World War.

The Holocaust Memorial

– a constant reminder that the Jews have always been a persecuted people.

● Holocaust Day, a day of commemoration, is observed in Israel on Nisan 27, and elsewhere on April 19 or 20. This is the anniversary of the beginning of the Warsaw Ghetto Uprising, when 60,000 unarmed Jews valiantly tried to resist deportation to the concentration and death camps.

● Gas chambers at Auschwitz, Majdanek, Treblinka, Chelmo, Sobibor and Belzec exterminated more than four million Jews.

'The Scream of the Mother' sculpture at Yad Vashem.

Jerusalem Today and Tomorrow

Even the most sceptical person can see how many of the Old Testament prophecies about Jerusalem and Israel have already been fulfilled.

The ingenuity of cultivating and irrigating stretches of former desert as citrus groves and fish farms is seen to fulfil the words of the prophet Isaiah: 'The desert and the parched land will be glad; the wilderness will rejoice and blossom. Like the crocus, it will burst into bloom; it will rejoice greatly and shout for joy' (Isaiah 35:1-2).

The fate of the Jews and the condition of Jerusalem are often referred to as 'barometers' of history by those who believe that the end of the world is tied up with the State of Israel, the return of the Jews to their homeland and to Jerusalem their capital.

The Jews still await the arrival of their Messiah in Zion. Many Christians believe that the conversion of Jews to the Christian faith will usher in the return of Jesus Christ as the culmination of history and the end of the world (see Romans 9-11). The apostle Paul writes that after 'the full number of Gentiles has come in . . . all Israel will be saved' (Romans 11:25-26).

Many Bible scholars, both Jewish and Christian, agree that the Old Testament prophetic visions see God's people, the Jews, in their land at the end of history. They are expected to return to their land and to worship God at Jerusalem (see Isaiah 27:13; Amos 9:11-15.)

The city of Jerusalem from the chapel of Dominus Flevit.

The beautiful prophecies of Zechariah picture what is now happening in Jerusalem: 'Once again men and women of ripe old age will sit in the streets of Jerusalem, each with cane in hand because of his age. The city streets will be filled with boys and girls playing there. . . . This is what the Lord Almighty says: "I will save my people from the countries of the east and the west. I will bring them back to live in Jerusalem"' (Zechariah 8:4-5, 7-8).

The Golden Gate, which is at present closed. Many believe that Jesus will enter it when he returns.

A prayer for Jerusalem

God of peace, you made Jerusalem the focus of your love for Israel; in Jerusalem you made peace with all mankind through the death and resurrection of Jesus.
We pray for all who live in this city, for whom in different ways it is a place of memories and hopes, of faith and anxiety.
May they find a peace in which people of different races and faiths may unite in trust and friendship.
May they find security based not on weapons but on justice and acceptance of each other.
In the name of Christ, who wept in love over this city and died in love outside its walls.

Facts to Remember

Heavenly Jerusalem

● The heavenly Jerusalem is where God's people will live, worshipping God and Jesus Christ in an eternal community.
● The book of Revelation pictures 'the Holy City, the new Jerusalem, coming down out of heaven from God, prepared as a bride beautifully dressed for her husband.'
● The prophecy continues: 'Now the dwelling of God is with men . . . He will wipe every tear from their eyes. There will be no more death or mourning or crying or pain' (Revelation 21:1-4).

Jerusalem and Prophecy

The Old Testament prophets look forward to a time when 'the fortunes of Judah and Jerusalem will be restored' (Joel 3:1):

● This will be a time when Jerusalem will not only be the political and religious centre for Israel, but for the whole world: 'the name of the Lord will be declared in Zion and his praise in Jerusalem when the peoples and the kingdoms assemble to worship the Lord' (Psalm 102:21-22).
● Many Orthodox Jews believe that we live 'in the last days', citing Isaiah's prophecy: 'Concerning Judah and Jerusalem: In the last days the mountain of the Lord's temple will be established as chief among the mountains; it will be raised above the hills, and all nations will stream to it' (Isaiah 2:2).

Index

Illustrations in *Italics*

Picture acknowledgements
All photographs by Tim Dowley and Peter Wyart (Tiger Colour Library), except p.18 (top), by Zev Radovan

Illustrations
Trevor Parkin: pp. 4-5, 18-19, 22-23
Jeremy Gower: p. 2
James Macdonald: pp. 6-7, 12-13
Richard Scott: pp. 6, 10, 19

Copyright © 1997
Three's Company/Angus Hudson Ltd

First published in the UK in 1997 by Candle Books Ltd.
Distributed by SP Trust, Triangle Business Park, Wendover Road, Aylesbury, Bucks HP22 5BL.
ISBN 185985 0820

Unless otherwise indicated, scripture quotations are from *The Holy Bible, New International Version*, copyright © 1973, 1978, 1984 by International Bible Society. Used by permission of Hodder & Stoughton. All rights reserved.
Quotations marked GNB are from the *Good News Bible, published by The Bible Societies/Harper Collins Publishers Ltd, UK*, © American Bible Society, 1966, 1971, 1976, 1992. The prayer on p. 31 is by Dr Stephen Travis, and reproduced with kind permission

Designed and created by Three's Company, 5 Dryden Street London WC2E 9NW

Enquiries to:
Angus Hudson Ltd,
Concorde House,
Grenville Place,
London NW7 3SA,
United Kingdom
Tel + 44 181 959 3668
Fax + 44 181 959 3678

Printed in Singapore